SCHOLASTIC

Trait-Based Writing
Graphic Organizers & Mini-Lessons

GRADES 2–4

JENNIFER JACOBSON

New York • Toronto • London • Auckland • Sydney
Mexico City • New Delhi • Hong Kong • Buenos Aires

Teaching *Resources*

Acknowledgments

Many thanks to Paula Flemming who ignited the writing flame

Teachers who wish to contact Jennifer about her staff development programs
may visit her Web site at www.jenniferjacobson.com.

Edited by Kathleen Hollenbeck
Cover design by Maria Lilja
Interior design by Holly Grundon
Interior illustrations by Teresa Anderko

ISBN-13: 978-0-439-57293-4
ISBN-10: 0-439-57293-2

Contents

Introduction 4

Connections to the Standards 6

References and Additional Resources 7

Mini-Lessons

Idea Treasure Map (*ideas and voice*) 8

Finding Focus (*ideas and organization*) 10

Choosing a Topic (*ideas*) 12

On Course (*ideas and voice*) 14

Personal Narrative Pond (*ideas, organization, and voice*) 16

Building a Story (*ideas and organization*) 18

Finding Your Voice (*ideas, voice, and word choice*) 20

Sharpen Your Writing Voice (*voice*) 22

Sensory Words (*word choice*) 24

Sentence Expansion Wheel (*sentence fluency*) 26

Picking Vivid Words (*word choice*) 28

Fluency Assessment (*voice, word choice, and sentence fluency*) 30

Sentence Fluency Checklist (*ideas and sentence fluency*) . . . 32

Show, Don't Tell! (*ideas and word choice*) 34

Editor's Organizer (*word choice, sentence fluency, and conventions*) . . . 36

Grand Slam Conventions! (*conventions*) 38

Fresh Words (*word choice*) 40

You're in the Movie! (*ideas and voice*) 42

Learning From Authors
(*ideas, organization, voice, word choice, sentence fluency, and conventions*) 44

Leap to New Ideas (*ideas and organization*) 46

Introduction

Welcome to *Trait-Based Writing Graphic Organizers & Mini-Lessons*! Designed for flexible use, these 20 graphic organizers boost the key writing skills emphasized in the Six-Traits + 1™ model. The organizers can be used to guide students in examining and exploring ideas, organization, voice, precise word choice, sentence fluency, and conventions and incorporating these traits in their writing. They also work well across genres from personal and fictional narratives to poetry, expository text, and persuasive speech to help students strengthen their composition skills in all areas.

Why Use Graphic Organizers to Teach Writing?

Graphic organizers provide schemata: a way of structuring information or arranging key concepts into a pattern, which forms the foundation for powerful, fluent writing (Bromley et al., 1995). Organizers offer students an efficient way to focus their attention, record facts and ideas, arrange and display their thinking, and monitor their use of writing strategies. The use of graphic organizers to organize and record their thinking before they write helps students plan the structure and direction of their ideas during the writing process. Graphic organizers are also useful in helping students assess and revise their writing for ideas, details, organization, word choice, voice, sentence fluency, and correct use of conventions.

Research has shown that graphic organizers:

* help students to integrate language and thinking in an organized format (Bromley et al, 1995).

* engage students in mid- to high-level thinking along Bloom's Taxonomy (comprehension, application, analysis, synthesis, and evaluation) (Dodge, 2005).

* help students distinguish between details that are important to know from those that may be interesting but are not essential (Ellis, 2004).

How to Use This Book

The organizers in this book can be used in any order and lend themselves well to many forms of teaching: pre- and post-assessment, preparation for writing assignments, and mini-lessons. They are suitable for use with the whole class, small groups, or individual students, and are ideal for long-term projects or independent written response.

The lessons are based on the writing traits and steps of the writing process as described in Ruth Culham's *6 + 1 Traits of Writing: The Complete Guide for the Primary Grades*. Each mini-lesson identifies the writing traits and processes that are addressed in the activity. A purpose states the uses and benefits of the activity, and the suggestion for introducing the lesson helps pique student interest. Step-by-step directions provide a guide for demonstrating how to use and complete the organizer. Also included is an activity that lets you take students a step further by building on the skills and strategies covered in the lesson or by using the organizer for a different purpose. Finally, to help you get started, the literature link suggests a book that might connect to or be appropriate for that particular lesson.

Using a Graphic Organizer

Select the graphic organizer that best suits your instructional needs. Then follow these suggestions to prepare and use the organizer with students.

✳ **Test It.** Before using an organizer, give it a "trial run" on your own to experience the process firsthand. This will allow you to see how well the graphic works with the selected text. Make any modifications necessary to best meet the needs of your students (Egan, 1999).

✳ **Present It.** Determine the best method for presenting the graphic organizer. You might make a photocopy for use as a transparency on the overhead projector, or distribute paper copies to students to complete as you model its use. Keep a supply of frequently used organizers on hand for students to use independently.

✳ **Model It.** Research has shown that graphic organizers are most effective when the teacher presents and models the organizer first for the whole group (Bowman et al., 1998). To ensure greatest success, model the use of each organizer with the whole class before asking students to complete it independently.

Helpful Hints for Success

✳ Model the use of the organizer so that students will gain a clear understanding of its purpose and how to complete it.

✳ Point out that planning before writing ensures a stronger, more focused, and more organized piece that will be easier for readers to follow and understand.

✳ Read aloud well-written picture books and excerpts from novels or chapter books to provide models of commendable writing.

✳ As often as possible, allow students freedom to choose their own topics. This will increase your students' engagement with their writing as well as their ability to generate and develop ideas.

✳ Provide specific and timely feedback of students' writing.

✳ Encourage students to read their work aloud—to the class, to a friend, or to themselves. Listening to one's work allows writers to identify lack of clarity, notice sentence fluency and voice, and catch conventional errors.

Assessing Student Performance

Graphic organizers are a performance-based model of assessment and are ideal for including in student portfolios, as they require students to demonstrate both their grasp of a concept and the thought process involved in writing about it. You can use the organizers in this book to determine how thoroughly students research a topic as well as how effectively they plan, organize, and treat information when writing about the topic. Organizers can also serve as a helpful tool for conferencing. For example, with You're in the Movie! (page 42), the student and teacher can form a clear view of words the student uses to create an image—and where further detail might be needed.

Students can also use graphic organizers to assess their own progress. For example, when completing Picking Vivid Words (page 28), students are asked to look at the word choice in a sample of their own writing and then replace targeted words with more vibrant ones.

Connections to the Standards

This book is designed to support you in meeting the following writing standards outlined by Mid-continent Research for Education and Learning (McREL), an organization that collects and synthesizes national and state standards.

Uses the general skills and strategies of the writing process.

* Prewriting: Uses prewriting strategies to plan written work (e.g., discusses ideas with peers, records reactions and observations).

* Drafting and Revising: Uses strategies to draft and revise written work (rereads; rearranges words, sentences, and paragraphs to improve or clarify meaning; varies sentence type; adds descriptive words and details; deletes extraneous information; incorporates suggestions from peers and teachers; sharpens the focus).

* Evaluates own and others' writing (asks questions and makes comments about writing; helps classmates apply grammatical and mechanical conventions).

* Uses strategies to organize written work (includes a beginning, middle, and ending; uses a sequence of events).

* Uses strategies (adapts focus, organization, point of view; determines knowledge and interests of audience) to write for different audiences (self, peers, teachers, adults).

* Uses strategies (adapts focus, point of view, organization) to write for a variety of purposes (to inform, entertain, explain, describe, record ideas).

* Writes expository, autobiographical, and expressive compositions (expresses ideas, reflections, and observations; uses narrative strategies, relevant details, and ideas that enable the reader to imagine the world of the event or experience).

* Writes narrative accounts, such as poems and stories.

Uses the stylistic and rhetorical aspects of writing.

* Uses descriptive words to convey basic ideas.

* Uses a variety of sentence structures in writing (expands basic sentence patterns; uses declarative, interrogative, exclamatory, and imperative sentences).

Uses grammatical and mechanical conventions in written compositions.

* Uses complete sentences in written compositions.

* Uses nouns, verbs, adjectives, adverbs, and coordinating conjunctions in written compositions.

Gathers and uses information for research purposes.

* Generates questions about topics of personal interest.

* Uses a variety of sources to gather information.

Kendall, J. S. & Marzano, R. J. (2004). *Content knowledge: A compendium of standards and benchmarks for K-12 education*. Aurora, CO: Mid-continent Research for Education and Learning. Online database: http://www.mcrel.org/standards-benchmarks/

References and Additional Resources

Bowman, L. A., Carpenter, J. & Paone, R. (1998). "Using graphic organizers, cooperative learning groups, and higher order thinking skills to improve reading comprehension." M.A. Action Research Project, Saint Xavier University. Chicago, IL.

Boyle, J. R. & Weishaar, M. (1997). "The effects of expert-generated vs. student-generated cognitive organizers on the reading comprehension of students with learning disabilities." *Learning Disabilities Research and Practice, 12* (4), 228–235.

Bromley, K., Irwin-De Vitis, L. & Modlo, M. (1995). *Graphic organizers: Visual strategies for active learning.* New York: Scholastic.

Bromley, K., Irwin-De Vitis, L. & Modlo, M. (1999). *50 Graphic organizers for reading, writing, and more.* New York: Scholastic.

Culham, R. (2001). *6 + 1 Traits of writing: The complete guide.* New York: Scholastic.

Dodge, J. (2005). *Differentiation in action.* New York: Scholastic.

Egan, M. (1999). "Reflections on effective use of graphic organizers." *Journal of Adolescent and Adult Literacy, 42* (8), 641.

Ellis, E. (2004). "Q & A: What's the big deal about graphic organizers?" www.graphicorganizers.com

Jacobson, J. (1999). *The big book of graphic organizers.* New York: Scholastic.

Moore, D. & Readence, J. (1984). "A quantitative and qualitative review of graphic organizer research." *Journal of Educational Research, 78* (1), 11–17.

Writing Traits

* Ideas
* Voice

Writing Process

* Prewriting

Literature Link

The Water Gift and the Pig of the Pig by Jacqueline Briggs Martin (Houghton Mifflin, 2003).

A lovely story about a girl, her grandfather, a beloved pig, and a special gift for finding water.

Idea Treasure Map

Purpose

Students mine their own memories for ideas by describing a favorite setting or recalling stories from their past.

Introducing the Activity

Ask students to close their eyes and sit quietly for a moment. Invite them to recall times and places in their past that brought them pleasure. Then have them open their eyes and begin the mini-lesson for the graphic organizer.

Using the Graphic Organizer

1. Choose a favorite childhood setting such as your backyard, grandmother's house, or favorite vacation spot. Draw a simple picture of the setting on the scroll on the graphic organizer. Describe attributes of the setting as you draw (for example, *"There was a small chicken coop in our yard"*).

2. Each time you include something in your drawing that reminds you of a personal event or experience (such as the porch steps your cat hid under during a blizzard), place an X on that part of the picture. Keep the memory to yourself for now, explaining that each X serves as a reminder of a situation that might make a good writing topic.

3. When you have finished drawing your picture, it will resemble a treasure map. Point to each X and tell about the event or experience that part of the drawing reminds you of. Then write the memory in a treasure chest. Tell students that now you have a treasury of ideas that you can write about in the future.

4. Distribute copies of the organizer for students to complete independently.

Taking It Further

Provide folders for students to store their completed organizers in. Have them refer to the treasure chests on their organizers whenever they need ideas for a personal writing topic.

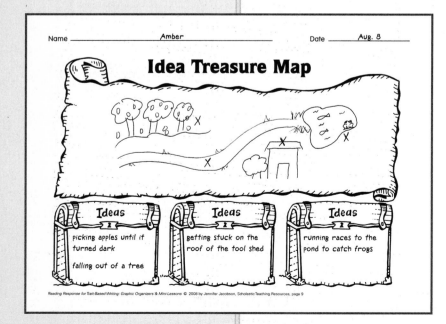

Name _____ Amber _____ Date ____ Aug. 8 ____

Idea Treasure Map

Ideas — picking apples until it turned dark / falling out of a tree

Ideas — getting stuck on the roof of the tool shed

Ideas — running races to the pond to catch frogs

Idea Treasure Map

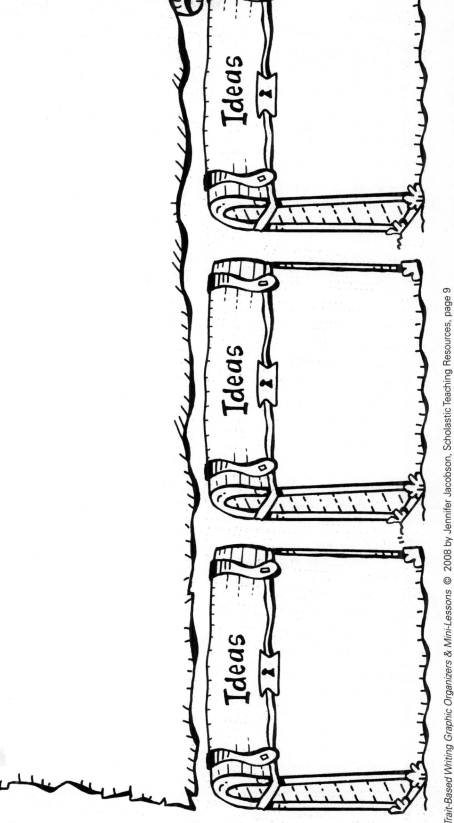

Writing Traits

* Ideas
* Organization

Writing Process

* Prewriting
* Drafting

Literature Link

Ste-e-e-e-eamboat-A-Comin'! by Jill Esbaum (Farrar, Straus and Giroux, 2005).

A village comes to life when a Mississippi River steamboat arrives and unloads its goods.

Finding Focus

Purpose

Students move from a general to specific topic, brainstorming details that bring clarity, originality, and voice to their writing.

Introducing the Activity

Invite students to help you brainstorm a list of broad categories, such as music, sports, and games. Write their suggestions on the board or on chart paper. Explain to students that details are essential in making their writing clear, expressing their own voice, and keeping their audience interested. Tell them that an effective way to do these things is to narrow down a general topic so that they focus on very specific details about it.

Using the Graphic Organizer

1. Distribute copies of the graphic organizer for students to complete as you guide the activity. Then have them select a topic from the list, such as "Games." Write the topic in the far left section of the telescope.

2. Ask students to narrow the topic by brainstorming more specific types of games, such as board games. Model how to write the new focus on the next section of the telescope.

3. Encourage students to narrow the topic even more by brainstorming specific kinds of board games. Have them write their own response on the third section of the telescope.

4. Invite students to share their personal experiences with the topic listed in the third section. This will help them narrow the topic further and make a specific, personal connection with it. For example, a student might respond, "One day, my sister and I played Monopoly all day long." Have students write their personal connection in the last section of the telescope.

5. Based on the narrower topic and personal experiences recorded on their telescopes, ask students to brainstorm related details they might want to include when writing about the topic. Have them record these details in the grass.

Taking It Further

Before writing, have students number each idea they plan to use. Explain that planning the order of story ideas in advance helps writers create text that flows and makes sense to readers.

Name _____ Ethan _____ Date _____ Aug. 14 _____

Finding Focus

Games | board games | Monopoly | One day, my sister and I played Monopoly all day long.

Details

It was raining. We stayed in our pajamas all day.

I wore cowboy pajamas.

I picked the shoe for my game marker.

My sister won piles and piles of money!

Reading Response for Trait-Based Writing: Graphic Organizers & Mini-Lessons © 2008 by Jennifer Jacobson, Scholastic Teaching Resources, page 11

Name _____

Date _____

Finding Focus

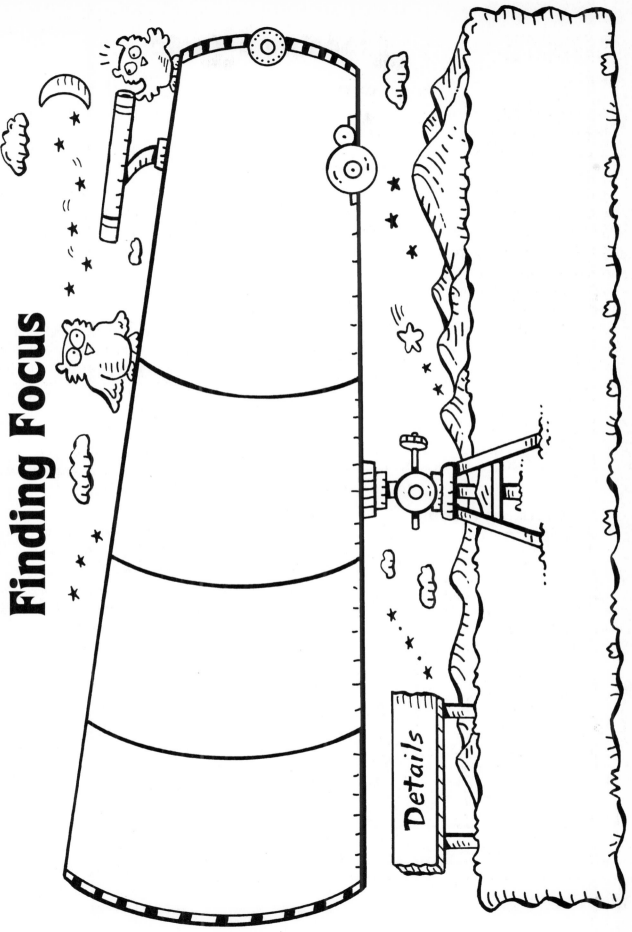

Details

* Ideas

Writing Process

* Prewriting
* Drafting

Literature Link

Crows: Strange and Wonderful by Laurence Pringle (Boyds Mills Press, 2002).

Use this excellent overview of crows and their amazing behaviors to demonstrate that "one bird" is a manageable topic.

Choosing a Topic

Purpose

Students examine topics to find one that is neither too limited nor too complicated to write about.

Introducing the Activity

Rather than asking students to generate topics they'd like to write about, ask them to suggest topics they'd like to *read* about. Invite them to tell what interests or intrigues them and what they'd be happy to read or edit during peer editing time. List these topics on the board as students name them.

Using the Graphic Organizer

1. Distribute copies of the graphic organizer. Then work with students to choose a topic from the class-generated list, such as "weather." Have them write that topic in the center gumball on their organizer.

2. Ask students to brainstorm six subtopics of the selected topic and then record these in the gumballs that immediately surround the main topic.

3. Have students think of things relating to each subtopic. Ask them to write their ideas in the gumballs that are connected by arrows to the subtopic.

4. After students fill in as many gumballs as possible, observe that there are far too many ideas to include in one essay or report. Together, choose one subtopic to write about. Ask: *Are there enough ideas springing from that subtopic to write about? If not, what other subtopic provides more connections?* Guide students to choose a subtopic that includes enough ideas with which to write an interesting paper.

Taking It Further

Try choosing a topic that is fairly unfamiliar to students. Ask them to brainstorm and record what they know about the topic on the organizer. Then have them research the topic to find new subtopics and ideas to add. Afterward, students can choose one of the subtopics and the related ideas to write about.

Name _____ Elizabeth _____   Date ___ Sept. 7 ___

Choosing a Topic

Write the main topic in the center gumball and subtopics in the other gumballs.

blizzard · high waves · wind · snowflakes · snow · thunder storms · hurricane · funnel cloud · rain · Main Topic: Weather · floods · tornado · strong winds · sleet · sun · dry · freezing rain · pellets · hot

The subtopic I will focus on is:

snow

Trait-Based Writing Graphic Organizers & Mini-Lessons © 2008 by Jennifer Jacobson, Scholastic Teaching Resources, page 13

Name _____   Date _____

Choosing a Topic

Write the main topic in the center gumball and
subtopics in the other gumballs.

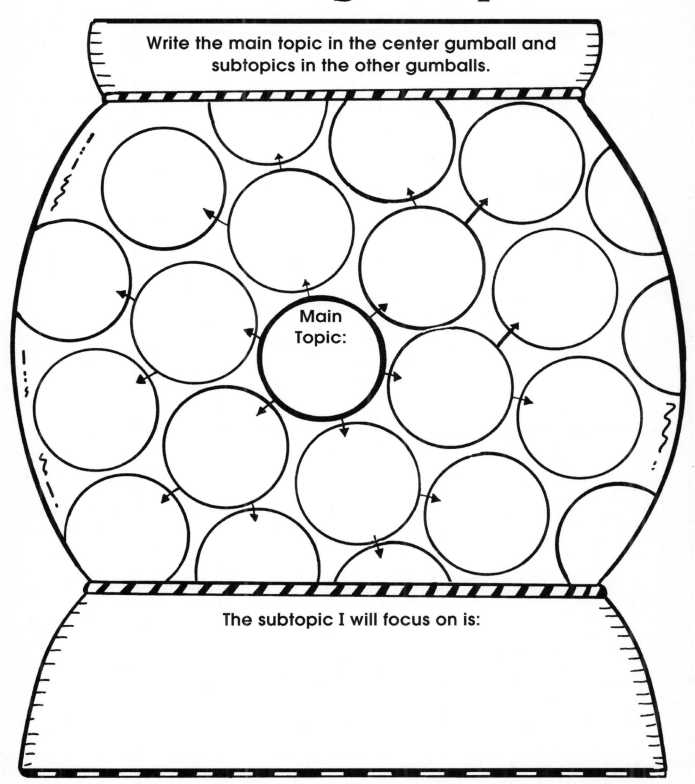

Main
Topic:

The subtopic I will focus on is:

Writing Traits

* Ideas
* Voice

Writing Process

* Prewriting
* Drafting
* Revising
* Sharing

Literature Link

*It Came from Beneath the Bed:
Tales from the House of Bunnicula*
by James Howe (Aladdin, 2003).

With the aid of Uncle Harold, Howie
the dachshund writes his own
exciting tale.

On Course

Purpose

Students examine their own writing to determine its appropriateness for the intended audience and clarity of content.

Introducing the Activity

Explain that since most writing is intended for an audience, authors work to present text that is organized, easy to read and understand, and interesting or appealing to the reader. Invite students to generate a list of possible audiences, such as parents, teachers, classmates, young children, teenagers, and so on. Tell them that writing for one audience may differ from that of writing for another audience. Invite students to share their ideas about why and to give examples of text that might be appropriate for the different kinds of audiences.

Using the Graphic Organizer

1. Have students select a topic to write about and decide who their audience will be (they might refer to the class-generated list for ideas). Distribute copies of the graphic organizer. Then explain that as you model how to complete it, students will fill in their own copies of the organizer.

2. Fill in the audience for your writing on the rooftop of the building. Then record what you want the reader to know—the main idea of your writing—on the penthouse.

3. Allow time for students to write a first draft for their topic. Then have them read over their text. Ask: *Is your writing appropriate for your intended audience? Did you tell readers what you want them to know? Is any information missing? Is there more information than needed?*

4. Have students write information they need to add on the up elevator and any they want to delete on the down elevator. Then have them revise their text.

5. Explain that receiving peer feedback can help students make decisions that will improve their writing. Invite them to share their revised work with peers and then discuss any changes suggested by their peers.

Taking It Further

After completing several organizers, have students review them to see if their additions and/or deletions demonstrate a pattern.

Name _____Mathew_____ Date __Sept. 19__

On Course

The audience for this piece is:

my class

What I want the reader to know most is . . .
my mother experienced an earthquake
when she was young.

Add

what my mother
did when she felt
the house shaking

the details of the
damage to her
house

Delete

where my mother
was born

pets that she didn't
have during the
earthquake

Trait-Based Writing Graphic Organizers & Mini-Lessons © 2008 by Jennifer Jacobson, Scholastic Teaching Resources, page 15

On Course

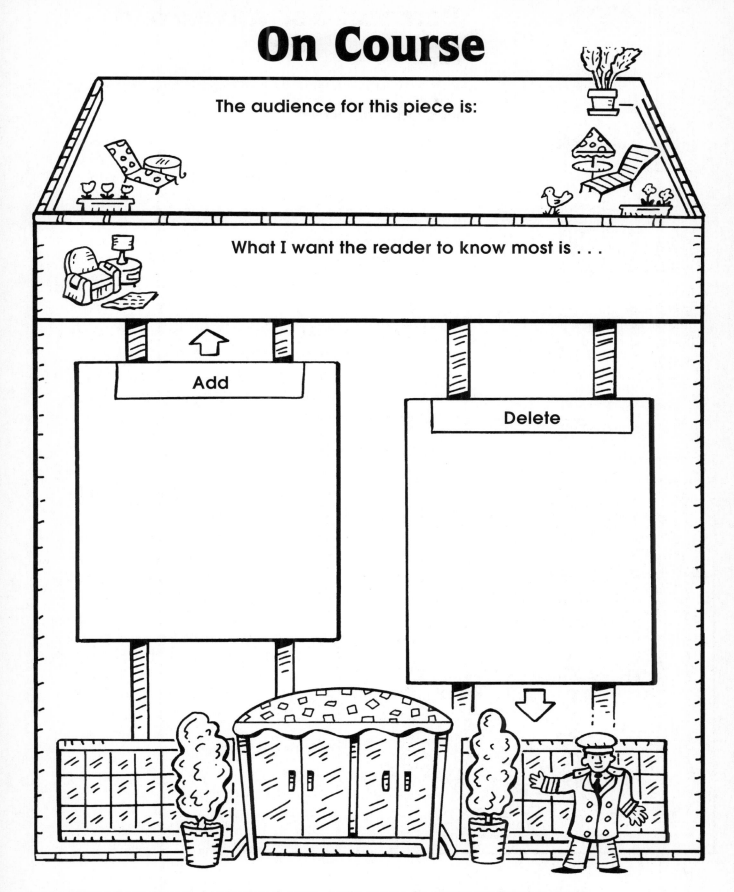

The audience for this piece is:

What I want the reader to know most is . . .

Add

Delete

Writing Traits

* Ideas
* Organization
* Voice

Writing Process

* Prewriting
* Drafting

Literature Link

Peach Heaven by Yangsook Choi (Farrar, Straus and Giroux, 2005).

When the sky begins to rain peaches, Yangsook finds herself in peach heaven. That is, until she realizes she must help the farmers who have lost their harvest.

Personal Narrative Pond

Purpose

Students create unique personal narratives.

Introducing the Activity

To demonstrate the difference between a generic topic and a specific, defined topic, print "Write about your favorite holiday" on the board. Invite students to comment on the topic and share reasons why this might be a difficult writing topic to tackle. Then write one or all of the following prompts on the board, again inviting student comments:

* Write about a time when you participated in a Halloween costume contest or parade.

* Write about how you swap Halloween treats with others to get the goodies you want.

* Write about a time you missed trick-or-treating because of the weather, an illness, or some other reason.

After sharing, explain that when a topic is narrowed down to a more specific idea—especially one to which students have personal connections—the easier it is to write about.

Using the Graphic Organizer

1. Distribute copies of the graphic organizer. Then provide students with a generic writing prompt, such as "Best Friends," to write on the frog.

2. Ask students to brainstorm four specific ideas about the topic that relate to their own experiences. Have them write each idea on a lily pad.

3. Have students choose an idea on one of the lily pads to write a personal narrative about. As they plan for writing, guide them to jot down ideas for their introduction, at least three events in the order they took place, and how they want to conclude their narrative. After organizing their ideas, have students write the first draft and then set it aside to review and revise at a later time.

Taking It Further

As a class, brainstorm a list of ten generic topics. Then challenge students by setting a timer for ten minutes and having them generate four ideas per topic that could be intriguing and unique to write about in a personal essay.

Name _____ Rachel _____ Date ___ Spet. 26 ___

Personal Narrative Pond

Idea: Tess and I had a big fight, but we made up.

Idea: Tess and I are different even though we are best friends.

Topic: Best Friends

Idea: Tess stood up for me so I could play in the softball game.

Idea: I have a treehouse that only my best friend Tess can come into.

Reading Response for Trait-Based Writing: Graphic Organizers & Mini-Lessons © 2008 by Jennifer Jacobson, Scholastic Teaching Resources, page 17

Personal Narrative Pond

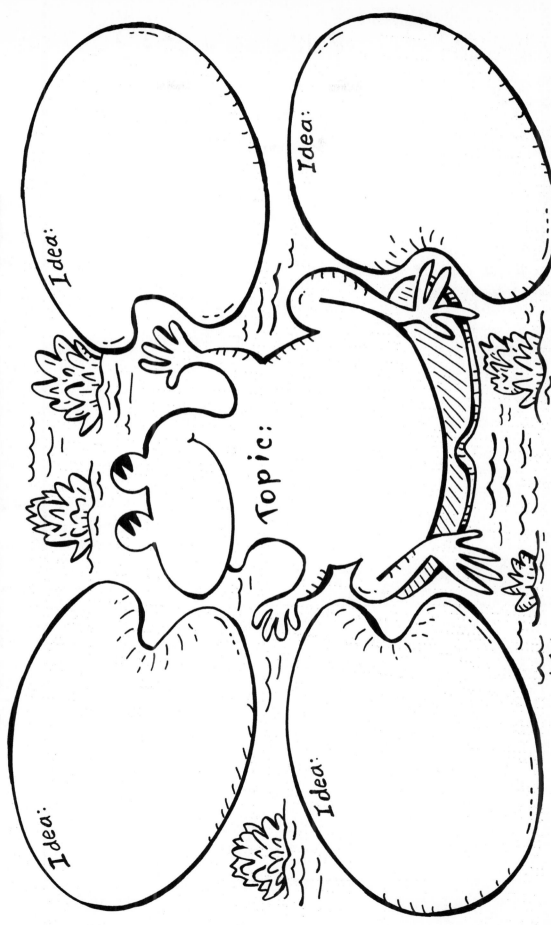

Idea:

Idea:

Idea:

Idea:

Topic:

Writing Traits
* Ideas
* Organization

Writing Process
* Prewriting
* Drafting

Literature Link

Horace and Morris Join the Chorus (but what about Dolores?) by James Howe (Aladdin 2005).

When Dolores doesn't make the chorus, she writes a persuasive letter to Moustro Provolone, the choral director.

Building a Story

Purpose

Students organize ideas and events to create a satisfying story.

Introducing the Activity

Tell students that most stories share this common pattern:

* a character wants something
* the character tries to get what he or she wants
* the character faces one or more obstacles or conflicts
* in the process, the character succeeds or is transformed in some way

Afterward, discuss how this pattern applies to a familiar story character, such as Stanley in *Holes* by Louis Sachar.

Using the Graphic Organizer

1. Read aloud a familiar story, such as James Howe's *Horace and Morris Join the Chorus.*

2. Work with students to choose a character who faces obstacles in obtaining something he or she wants. Fill in the character's name on the graphic organizer. Then record what the character wanted and what he or she did to try to get what was wanted.

3. Ask students to identify the obstacle or conflict that prevents the character from succeeding. Record this information in the column labeled "But..." Then summarize the plot up to that point, using "but" to demonstrate how it fits into the scheme (for example, "Dolores auditioned for the chorus, *but* she didn't make the cut."

4. Have students tell what happened to allow the character to succeed or cause him or her to change. Write their response in the "So..." column, explaining that this is the resolution, or conclusion. Again, provide a summary, such as "*So* Dolores wrote a letter to the director and he agreed to teach her to sing."

5. Distribute copies of the organizer for students to use to create ideas for their own stories. As they write, encourage them to try to keep to the "But-So" pattern.

Taking It Further

Invite students to replace information on the chart with their own ideas to explore how they might rewrite the story to make it their own.

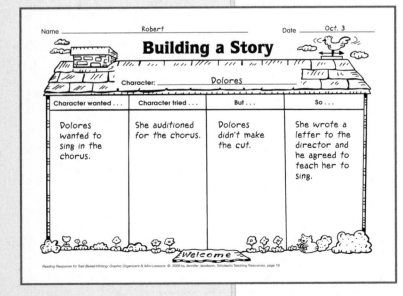

Name _____ Robert _____ Date ____ Oct. 3 ____

Building a Story

Character: _____ Dolores _____

Character wanted ...	Character tried ...	But ...	So ...
Dolores wanted to sing in the chorus.	She auditioned for the chorus.	Dolores didn't make the cut.	She wrote a letter to the director and he agreed to teach her to sing.

Welcome

Reading Response for Trait-Based Writing: Graphic Organizers & Mini-Lessons © 2008 by Jennifer Jacobson, Scholastic Teaching Resources, page 18

Name —————

Date —————

Building a Story

Character: —————

Character wanted	Character tried	But	So . . . .

Welcome

Writing Traits

✳ Ideas
✳ Voice
✳ Word Choice

Writing Process

✳ Prewriting
✳ Drafting

Literature Link

Boris and Bella by Carolyn Crimi (Voyager Books, 2006).

Messy Bella Legrossi and picky Boris Kleanitoff discover they can agree on some things. Voice galore!

Finding Your Voice

Purpose

Students recognize that their individual ways of thinking, unique descriptions, and quirky expressions add up to a strong and lively voice.

Introducing the Activity

Invite students to think about their family life—and what makes their family members unique and fun to be with. Are there expressions, shared jokes, or peculiar habits within the household? Invite volunteers to share a few with the class.

Using the Graphic Organizer

1. Provide students with a writing prompt that focuses on their own experiences, such as a family gathering, school activity, or sporting or extracurricular event. For example, you might highlight family idiosyncrasies with a prompt such as "If a stranger joined you and your family for dinner, how might he or she describe the experience?"

2. Distribute copies of the graphic organizer. Have students record the topic and then brainstorm words, phrases, or expressions that come to mind when they think about the prompt.

3. Following the prompts on the organizer, have students record adjectives, attitudes, words or phrases, and opinions that describe their family time. For example, under "Personal Dictionary," a student might write, *"Stop killing the table fairies"* as his or her family's code phrase for *"Take your elbows off the table."* Remind students that unique details and feelings about an experience create *voice*. The more specific their observations and memories of the experience, the stronger their unique writing voice will be.

4. Invite students to write about the topic, incorporating ideas from their completed organizer.

Taking It Further

This organizer offers a great opportunity for a home-school connection. Once students know how to fill out the organizer, encourage them to involve their families in completing it at home.

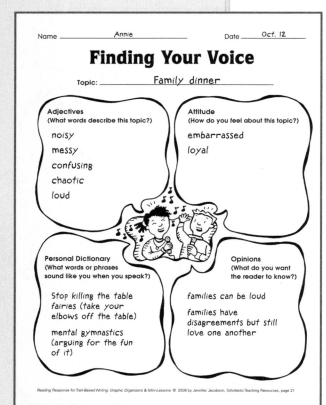

Name _____   Date _____

Finding Your Voice

Topic: _____

Adjectives
(What words describe this topic?)

Attitude
(How do you feel about this topic?)

Personal Dictionary
(What words or phrases
sound like you when you speak?)

Opinions
(What do you want
the reader to know?)

Writing Traits

✻ Voice

Writing Process

✻ Prewriting
✻ Drafting
✻ Revising

Literature Link

Rain Romp by Jane Kurtz
(Greenwillow, 2002).

This lyrical story of a girl who wakes
up feeling grouchy provides many
opportunities to discuss the ways in
which authors express voice.

Sharpen Your Writing Voice

Purpose

Students recognize voice in writing, identify strategies that contribute to this trait, and write using their own voice.

Introducing the Activity

Read aloud short poems written by three different authors, such as Jack Prelutsky, Robert Frost, and Maya Angelou. Afterward, help students identify the poet's tone or voice. For example, Prelutsky uses humor, Frost focuses on nature and life's difficult choices, and Angelou speaks from the heart in her verse. Point out how these poets used their voice to make uniquely significant contributions to literature.

Using the Graphic Organizer

1. Distribute copies of the graphic organizer. Then help students search the classroom library for examples of voice in writing.

2. After making their selection, have students record a brief passage from it on the section of a pencil labeled "Example of voice." (You might also have them include the title of the selection and page number on which the passage is found.)

3. Ask students to share ways in which their passage expresses voice. Responses might include:

    ✻ the writing shows enthusiasm

    ✻ you can tell that the author likes her or his subject

    ✻ the writing has "attitude"

    ✻ the author's words express feeling

    ✻ words show a different way of looking at the topic

   Afterward, have students record on the pencil some ways that the author creates voice.

4. Have students repeat steps 2 and 3 to fill in the other pencil.

5. Encourage students to incorporate some of the mentioned strategies to express voice in their own writing.

Taking It Further

Have students use the organizer to examine examples of voice in their own writing and how they created it. Then help them identify ways they might make their voice more expressive and memorable.

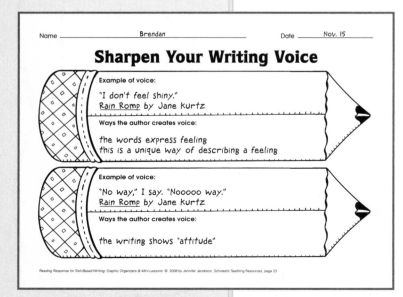

Name _____ Brendan _____ Date ___ Nov. 15 ___

Sharpen Your Writing Voice

Example of voice:

"I don't feel shiny."
Rain Romp by Jane Kurtz

Ways the author creates voice:

the words express feeling
this is a unique way of describing a feeling

Example of voice:

"No way," I say. "Nooooo way."
Rain Romp by Jane Kurtz

Ways the author creates voice:

the writing shows "attitude"

Sharpen Your Writing Voice

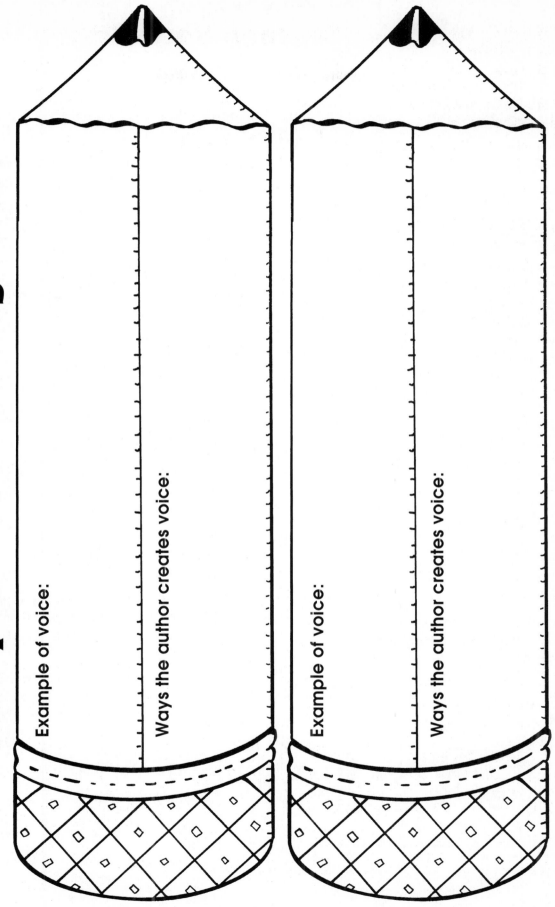

Example of voice:

Ways the author creates voice:

Example of voice:

Ways the author creates voice:

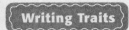

Writing Traits

* Word Choice

Writing Process

* Prewriting
* Drafting
* Revising

Literature Link

The Boy Who Drew Birds by Jacqueline Davies (Houghton Mifflin, 2004).

A well-crafted biography of John Audubon revealing that he was the first to band birds' legs to determine their migration patterns.

Sensory Words

Purpose

Students focus on writing with words that tap into the senses.

Introducing the Activity

Label a large five-column chart with the five senses: taste, touch, sight, smell, and sound. After reviewing the senses, invite students to brainstorm descriptive words that bring each sense to life, such as *spicy* for taste, *gritty* for touch, and *piercing* for sound. (Encourage them to go beyond conventional words, such as *sweet* and *salty,* and reach for more descriptive words that define specific sensory experiences.) Write their responses on the chart. When finished, tell students that successful writers often use words that tap into the five senses to create text that helps readers feel as if they personally experience the story.

Using the Graphic Organizer

1. Distribute copies of the graphic organizer. Have students fill in the name of a setting, such as a kitchen.

2. Invite students to brainstorm sights, sounds, smells, tastes, and physical sensations they associate with the setting. For example, in a kitchen, they might smell cookies baking, dishwashing detergent in use, or sour odors around the trashcan. Model how to record the sensations on the appropriate cookies on your own copy of the organizer. Have students fill in their cookies.

3. Review student responses, one cookie at a time. Invite them to share additional information about their responses and to add other sensations, if desired.

4. Ask students to write a description of the setting, using sensory words from their organizer to help make the setting come to life.

5. Have students share their writing with peers to get feedback on the effectiveness of their word choice. Later, have them revise their work based on peer suggestions and their own assessment of the first draft.

Taking It Further

Have students take the organizer home to record sights, sounds, tastes, sights, and physical sensations of a specific part of their home or other setting outside of school.

Name _____ Thomas _____   Date ____ NOv. 20 ____

Sensory Words

Setting: _____ kitchen _____

Words you can "see"

shiny pans
rising dough
melting butter

Words you can "touch"

slippery dishes
soft, gooey dough
crunchy cookies

Words you can "hear"

timer ticking
clink of dishes
splash!

Words you can "smell"

cookies baking
dishwashing detergent
sour trash

Words you can "taste"

cold, fresh milk
sugary cookies

Reading Response for Trait-Based Writing: Graphic Organizers & Mini-Lessons © 2008 by Jennifer Jacobson, Scholastic Teaching Resources, page 25

Sensory Words

Setting:

Words you can "hear"

Words you can "taste"

Words you can "touch"

Words you can "see"

Words you can "smell"

Writing Traits

* Sentence Fluency

Writing Process

* Prewriting
* Drafting

Literature Link

Wolf! Wolf! by John Rocco
(Hyperion, 2007).

An entertaining retelling of the
boy who cried wolf—from the
wolf's point of view.

Sentence Expansion Wheel

Purpose

Students include more information to expand and refine sentences.

Introducing the Activity

Explain that a single sentence can hold a great deal of information. To strengthen students' understanding of what constitutes a strong sentence, write "Yesterday, the plumber came to our house to fix broken pipes" on the board. Read the sentence aloud and then ask:

"Who *is the sentence about?*"   "When *did he fix the pipes?*"

"What *did the plumber do?*"   "Why *did he fix the pipes?*"

"Where *did he fix the pipes?*"

Using the Graphic Organizer

1. Distribute copies of the graphic organizer. Ask students to write a short sentence, such as "We walked" on the pipe at the top left.

2. Explain that students will answer each question on the water wheel to provide more information about the short sentence. Point out that their answers might be single words or phrases, and the questions might be interpreted in various ways as they relate to students' answers to other questions on the wheel. For instance, one student might interpret "Why?" as "Why did we walk to the playground?" while another interprets it as "Why did we walk quickly?" Have students record each answer on the corresponding section.

3. Encourage students to form a longer sentence from the short one, incorporating as many of their answers as possible. For example, one student might create the sentence "On Saturday, my brother and I walked quickly to the playground so we could play on the seesaw" while another comes up with "Last week, my friend and I walked barefooted on the beach." Have students write their expanded sentence in the water at the bottom of the page.

4. Write the sentences on the board as students share them. Point out how their sentences differ in both content and structure. Then tell students that varying sentence structures adds interest and helps make their writing flow.

Taking It Further

Encourage students to choose a short sentence from their own writing and then use the organizer to expand it.

Name ___Austin___   Date ___Dec. 7___

Sentence Expansion Wheel

Short Sentence:
We walked.

Who: my brother and I

How: quickly

Where: to the playground

Why: we wanted to play on the seesaw

When: Saturday

Expanded Sentence:

On Saturday, my brother and I walked quickly to the playground so we could play on the seesaw.

Reading Response for Trait-Based Writing: Graphic Organizers & Mini-Lessons © 2008 by Jennifer Jacobson, Scholastic Teaching Resources, page 27

Name ——————————— Date ———————————

Sentence Expansion Wheel

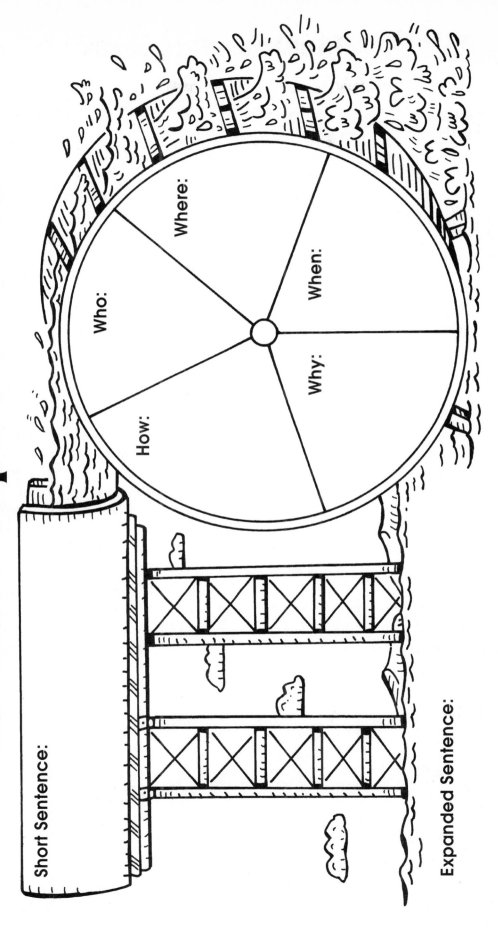

Short Sentence:

Who:

Where:

How:

When:

Why:

Expanded Sentence:

* Word Choice

Writing Process

* Sharing
* Revising

Literature Link

Harry Potter and the Sorcerer's Stone by J. K. Rowling (Scholastic, 1998).

Although ignored and mistreated in the world of humans, Harry Potter finds fame and adventure at the Hogwarts School of Witchcraft.

Picking Vivid Words

Purpose

Students explore word choice by replacing general or nonspecific words with more precise, descriptive words.

Introducing the Activity

Explain that students will work with partners to review a sample of their own writing to discover ways to improve word choice. Have students select an earlier written assignment to use for this activity.

Using the Graphic Organizer

1. Distribute a copy of the graphic organizer to each student. Ask students to take turns reading the selected writing aloud to their partner.

2. After reading, have the partners review the text to find and circle words they think are ineffective or could be replaced with more accurate or interesting words. Ask them to highlight the five most critical words. When finished, instruct the author to record each of the five words on a flower on the organizer.

3. Working together, encourage the partners to brainstorm other words for each targeted word, trying to come up with more precise or interesting words that might be used to replace the original word. Have the author list the new words on each flower. For example, for the original word *went*, the pair might list possible replacement words such as *raced, strolled, hurried,* or *marched.* If students need more space, have them also write words on other parts of the flowers.

4. After reviewing both writing samples, have the partners revise their own work, replacing each targeted ineffective word with a more effective, precise word from the corresponding flower. While revising, students might also find and replace other instances of ineffective words.

5. Once again, invite the partners to share their writing, taking time to discuss whether the new word choices are more effective than the original words.

Taking It Further

Provide examples of vibrant text found in published works, such as in *Harry Potter and the Sorcerer's Stone* by J. K. Rowling. Have students identify words in the example that make it interesting and bring it to life.

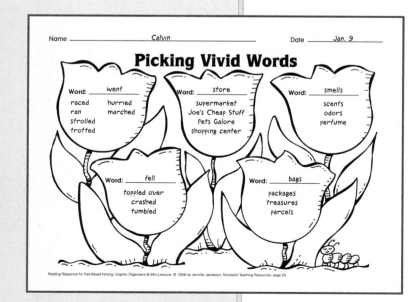

Name _____

Date _____

Picking Vivid Words

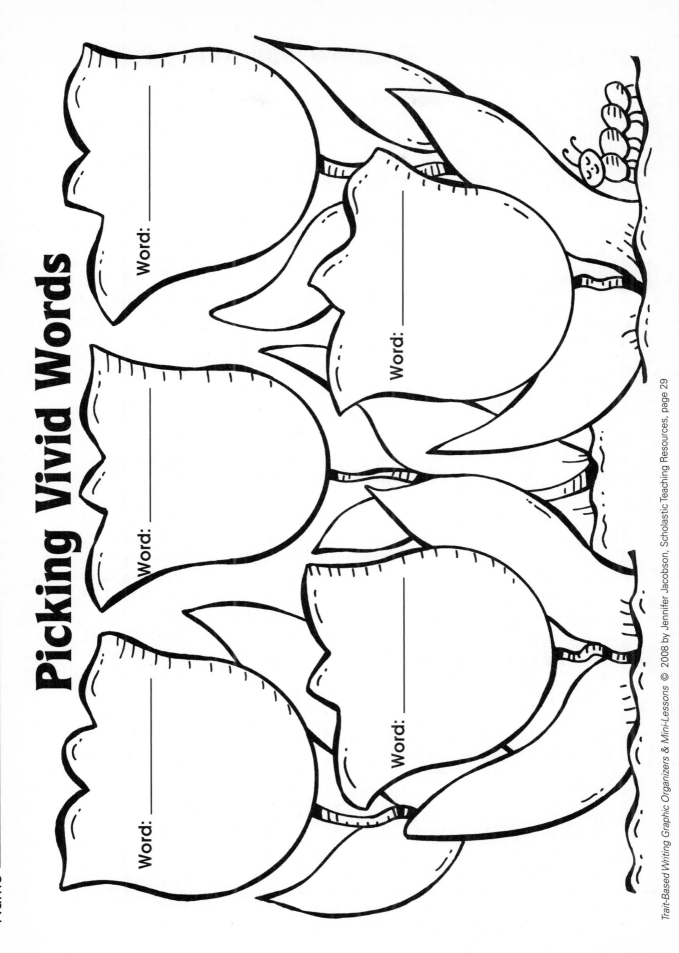

Word: _____

Word: _____

Word: _____

Word: _____

Fluency Assessment

Purpose

Students examine their writing to find and justify the use of simple and complex sentences.

Introducing the Activity

Read aloud a passage from a familiar story, such as the beginning of chapter 3 in *Charlotte's Web* by E. B. White. Point out the different sentence lengths and ask: *Why do you think authors sometimes use short, simple sentences?* Students might share ideas such as "to emphasize a point," "to create a quick pace," or "to mimic realistic dialogue." Then ask: *Why do authors use longer, more complicated sentences?* Responses might include "to provide a detailed description," "to make a comparison with a simile or metaphor," or "to portray action." Finally, tell students that authors often vary sentence length in their writing to create appealing, fluent text.

Using the Graphic Organizer

1. Select a draft of students' writing for them to use for this activity. Then distribute copies of the graphic organizer.

2. Explain that students will examine and evaluate the sentences in their writing. Ask them to find examples of both long and short sentences in their text. Have them copy a sentence in each row in the "Sentence" column on the chart.

3. Ask students to read each sentence and check the box that best indicates its length. Then have them read each sentence in context and examine it by asking questions such as: *What was my intent in using this sentence? Did I need more words to describe greater detail? Did I want to get the reader's attention by using a shorter sentence? Why else might I have chosen to use a sentence of this length here?* Have students fill in the "Why?" column with one or more reasons for using a sentence of that length in their passage.

4. Encourage students to use the information on their organizers to revise their writing, shortening or lengthening sentences throughout the text to improve fluency.

Taking It Further

Instruct students to compose a short paragraph, using the organizer to document the length of each sentence and their reason for choosing that length.

Name _____ Hannah _____ Date _____ Jan. 16 _____

Fluency Assessment

Sentence	Short	Long	Why?
Tess and I were on the same softball team, but we had never met.		✓	to give detail and background information
I caught the ball, spun around, and flipped it into Tess's glove.		✓	to describe a series of actions
Tess froze.	✓		to build suspense
The runner was out!	✓		for emphasis and impact

Name _____

Date _____

Fluency Assessment

Sentence	Short	Long	Why?

Writing Traits

* Ideas
* Sentence Fluency

Writing Process

* Sharing
* Revising

Literature Link

Spiders and Their Webs by Darlyne A. Murawski (National Geographic Children's Books, 2004).

This spectacular book features nine types of spiders and their webs, with captivating descriptions, useful facts, and stunning photographs.

Sentence Fluency Checklist

Purpose

Students evaluate their own and classmates' writing to increase their understanding and use of sentence fluency.

Introducing the Activity

To demonstrate what is meant by sentence fluency, explain the following keys to fluency, providing examples from a familiar story as needed:

* sentences vary in length
* sentences have different beginnings
* sentences flow together meaningfully (with the help of transitional words and phrases where needed)
* words are precise and interesting (no unnecessary words are present)
* dialogue sounds natural

Using the Graphic Organizer

1. Select a draft of students' writing for them to use for this activity. Distribute copies of the graphic organizer and have students fill in the title of their writing.

2. Review the five keys, using the list in the left column as a guide. Then have students read their own writing, thinking about each key as they read and deciding whether or not it is true for their text. If true, have them check the box next to the key. If not, have them write NR for "Needs Revision."

3. After evaluating their own work, help students staple together their organizer and writing sample. Then divide them into groups of four. Tell students that they will now read and evaluate the writing sample for each member of their group. Have the group members exchange their work. For each writing sample, ask students to write their name in the "Reviewer" row and then read and evaluate the work by filling in the boxes under their name.

4. After the organizers are completed, have students retrieve their own writing samples and use the information on the organizer to make revisions.

Taking It Further

Have students use the organizer to review several drafts of their own writing. They can use the information to track their progress and note patterns or areas needing improvement.

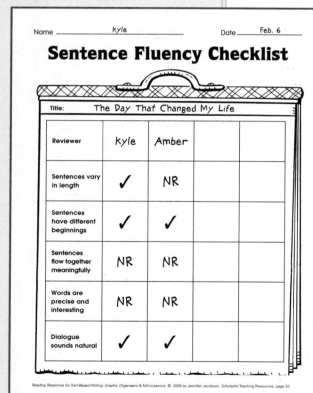

Name _____ Kyle _____   Date _____ Feb. 6 _____

Sentence Fluency Checklist

Title: The Day That Changed My Life

Reviewer	Kyle	Amber		
Sentences vary in length	✓	NR		
Sentences have different beginnings	✓	✓		
Sentences flow together meaningfully	NR	NR		
Words are precise and interesting	NR	NR		
Dialogue sounds natural	✓	✓		

Reading Response for Trait-Based Writing: Graphic Organizers & Mini-Lessons © 2008 by Jennifer Jacobson, Scholastic Teaching Resources, page 33

Name _____   Date _____

Sentence Fluency Checklist

Title: _____

Reviewer				
Sentences vary in length				
Sentences have different beginnings				
Sentences flow together meaningfully				
Words are precise and interesting				
Dialogue sounds natural				

Literature Link

Truly Winnie by Jennifer Richard Jacobson (Houghton Mifflin, 2006).

Winnie's carefree days at camp become complicated as she watches a tiny fib rapidly grow into one not-so-little lie after another.

Show, Don't Tell!

Purpose

Students use words and phrase to imply meaning, rather than *telling* readers what they wish to convey.

Introducing the Activity

Have students close their eyes and imagine they are seeing a story they'd like to write come to life. Encourage them to try to visualize one or more scenes that include a character who is engaged in an activity, dialogue, or thinking process. (Visualize your own story while students imagine theirs.)

Using the Graphic Organizer

1. Distribute copies of the graphic organizer. As you model how to complete the organizer, have students fill in their own copies.

2. Write a summary of your visualized story on the top stripe of the kite. Have students also fill in their summaries, which might include something realistic (such as a goal realized) or fictitious (talking animals).

3. Ask: *What adjectives describe the character's emotions in your scene?* Name adjectives that apply to your own character, such as *disappointed, excited,* and *angry*. Write these on the middle stripe. Have students write their adjectives on their organizer.

4. Encourage students to try to convey their character's emotion without directly stating it (by avoiding using the adjectives they listed), but rather by describing actions that help readers visualize the emotions. For example, they might convey anger by describing their character folding his or her arms and stomping a foot. Have students record their descriptions in the bottom stripe.

5. Referring to their visualized scenes and the ideas on their kite, have students create sentences that *show* their character's emotions. Have them write each "showing" sentence on a kite tail. For example, rather than "Jean felt angry," a student might write, "Jean clenched her teeth, folded her arms, and stomped off."

Taking It Further

Ask students to search their reading materials to find examples where the author *shows*, rather than states, a character's emotions. Use these examples to help students explore how authors convey ideas through their choice of words.

Name _____ Bruce _____   Date _____ Feb. 22 _____

Show, Don't Tell!

Scene Summary:
Jean tries to ride her bike up a steep hill, but she keeps falling down or she can't pedal hard enough to make it.

Sentence:
Jean clenched her teeth, folded her arms, and stomped off.

Adjectives:
mad	frustrated
angry	disappointed
furious	

Sentence:
Jean fell to the ground and screamed.

Sentence:
Jean's face turned red as she fought back tears.

Actions:
crosses arms	screams
turns red	cries
stomps foot	kicks
stomps away	

Sentence:
Jean kicked the bike, stuck her tongue out at the hill, then walked toward home.

Show, Don't Tell!

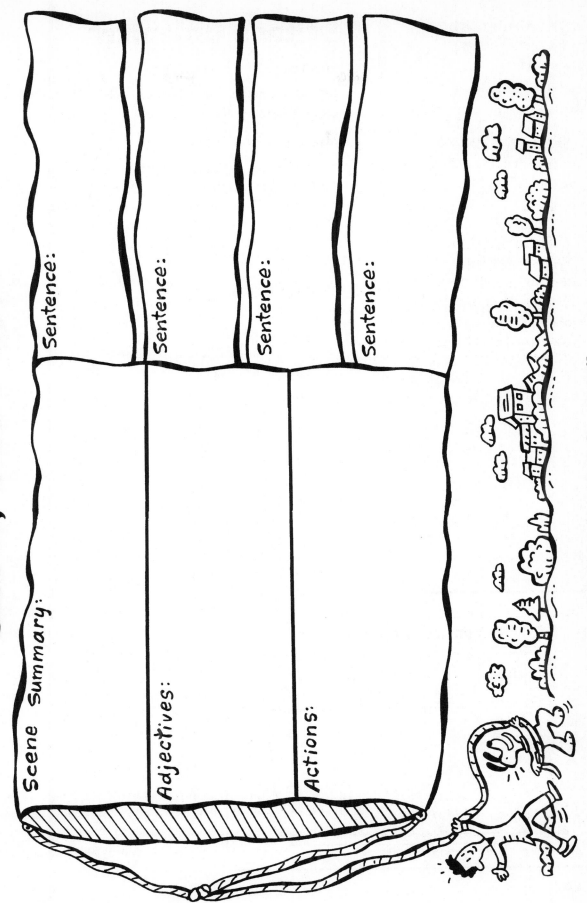

Scene Summary:

Adjectives:

Actions:

Sentence:

Sentence:

Sentence:

Sentence:

Writing Traits

* Word Choice
* Sentence Fluency
* Conventions

Writing Process

* Sharing
* Revising
* Editing

Literature Link

Punctuation Takes a Vacation by Robin Pulver (Holiday House, 2004).

When the punctuation marks in Mr. Wright's class take a vacation, students discover just how difficult life can be without them.

Editor's Organizer

Purpose

Students self- and peer-edit writing samples to target changes and corrections to consider during revisions.

Introducing the Activity

Ask for a show of hands from students who have experienced confusion or frustration after having an edited writing sample returned to them covered with marks and comments. Invite students to share problems they've encountered with trying to decode or make sense of the marks. Then tell them that they will learn a neater, more efficient and organized way to make edits.

Using the Graphic Organizer

1. Write a short story on chart paper, intentionally including spelling, grammar, and punctuation mistakes, as well as some poor word choices. Ask students to read the story to themselves, mentally noting the errors they encounter.

2. Display the graphic organizer on the overhead projector. Explain that you will use the labeled sections of the desk organizer to record editing notes, rather than marking on the writing sample.

3. To demonstrate, review your story one sentence at a time, inviting students to point out the errors. Number each error and have students identify what kind of error it is. For example, they should identify the incorrect use of a question mark as a Punctuation error. Write the error number and a brief note on the corresponding section of the organizer.

4. When finished, use the think-aloud method to model how to use the recorded information. For example, you might say: *On my paragraph, number one is marked over a period. That number is in the Punctuation section on the organizer. That means I need to check and correct the punctuation I used here.* Review all edits to demonstrate how the process works for all types of editing errors.

5. Distribute copies of the organizer for students to use to edit a sample of their own or a peer's writing.

Taking It Further

Have students use the completed organizer to correct and revise their writing sample. If working with a peer, invite the partners to discuss the edits before revising their work.

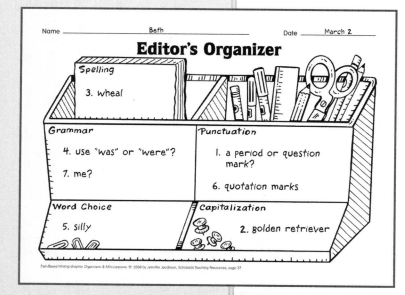

Name _____ Beth _____   Date _____ March 2 _____

Editor's Organizer

Spelling

   3. wheal

Grammar

   4. use "was" or "were"?

   7. me?

Punctuation

   1. a period or question mark?

   6. quotation marks

Word Choice

   5. silly

Capitalization

   2. golden retriever

Name _____

Date _____

Editor's Organizer

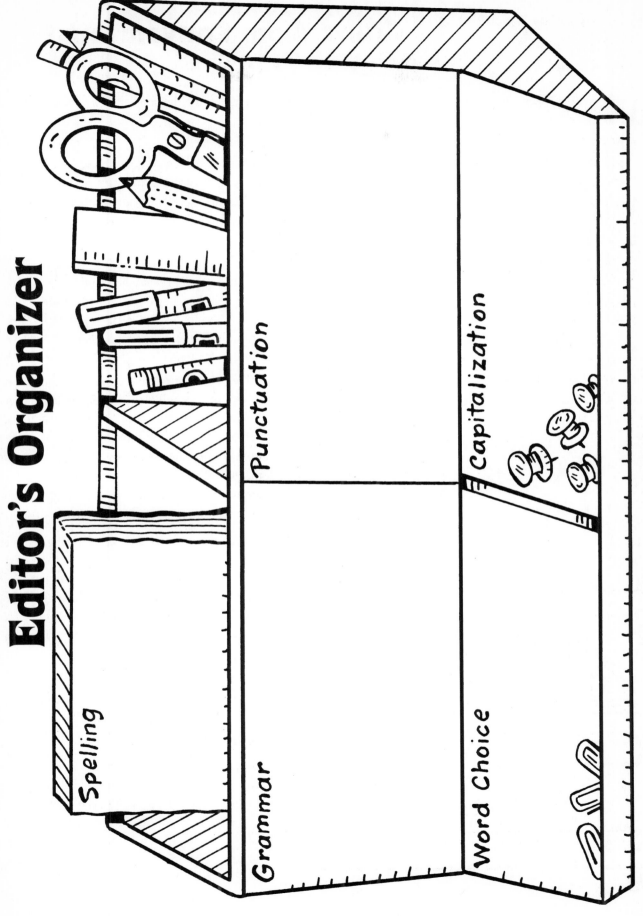

Spelling

Grammar

Punctuation

Word Choice

Capitalization

* Conventions

Writing Process

* Drafting
* Editing

Literature Link

Granny Torrelli Makes Soup
by Sharon Creech (HarperTrophy, 2005).

With the help of her wise old grandmother, Rosie manages to work out relationship problems with her best friend, Bailey.

Grand Slam Conventions!

Purpose

Students set personal goals for learning the conventions of writing.

Introducing the Activity

Tell students that writing conventions have to do with the mechanical correctness of written work: spelling, use of capitals, punctuation, grammar, and knowing when to start a new paragraph. Invite volunteers to share what they know about some of the conventions.

Using the Graphic Organizer

1. Display the graphic organizer. Explain that when students are "pitched" a writing convention that they don't know or understand, they can run it around the bases to develop a strategy to learn more about it. Then ask them to think about specific conventions they've encountered, but may not understand.

2. Invite students to share their observations and questions. Choose one of their responses, such as "I understand that commas are used when listing items, but I don't know whether to use a comma after the last item in the list." Record the category of the convention on the pitcher's mound (in this case, "Punctuation") and the observation ("commas are used when writing lists") on first base.

3. Move around the bases, reading each prompt, inviting student responses, and choosing one or more responses to write on the base.

4. When you reach home plate, discuss strategies students might use to help them learn what they need to know about the convention. For example, they might study examples in print or ask the teacher to learn about comma use in a series. Write one or more helpful strategies on the base.

5. Distribute copies of the organizer for students to complete independently. Encourage them to share what they know about different conventions with the class.

Taking It Further

Assign each student a common conventions problem, such as *"Do quotation marks come before or after the punctuation at the end of a sentence?"* Have students find the answer, write it on an index card, and then file it in a box to be used for future reference when writing.

Name _____ Zack _____   Date _____ March 15 _____

Grand Slam Conventions!

I already know:
commas go between the items in a list

I need to learn:
Does a comma follow the last item in the list?

Convention:
Punctuation

I have observed:
commas are used when writing lists

How I will learn it:
ask a teacher
study examples in books and magazines

Reading Response for Trait-Based Writing: Graphic Organizers & Mini-Lessons © 2008 by Jennifer Jacobson, Scholastic Teaching Resources, page 39

Name _____

Date _____

Grand Slam Conventions!

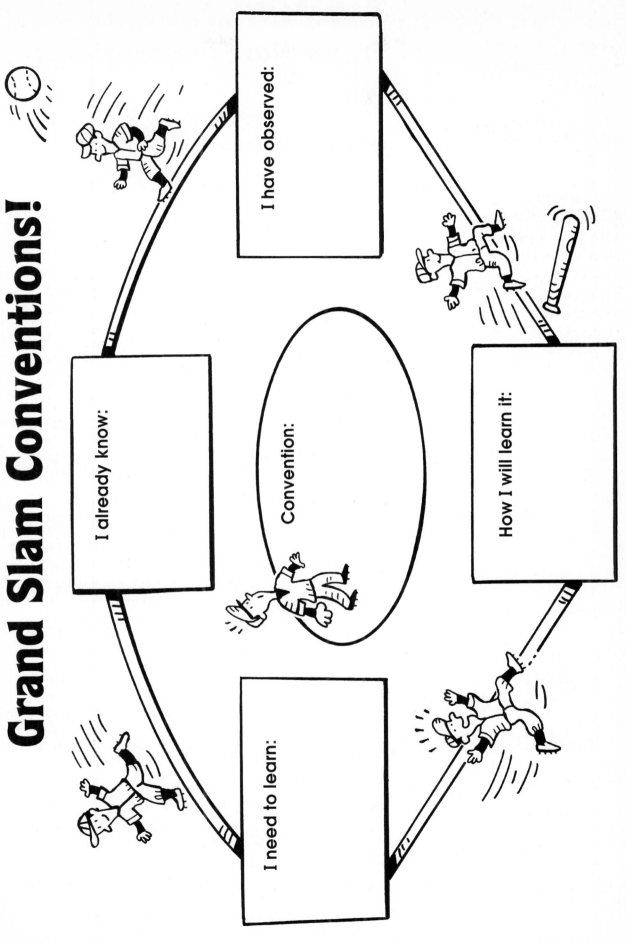

I have observed:

I already know:

Convention:

How I will learn it:

I need to learn:

Trait-Based Writing Graphic Organizers & Mini-Lessons © 2008 by Jennifer Jacobson, Scholastic Teaching Resources, page 39

* Word Choice

Writing Process

* Revising

Literature Link

Max's Words by Kate Banks (Farrar, Straus & Giroux, 2006).

When Max's brothers refuse to share their stamp and coin collections, Max decides to start a collection of his own—a word collection!

Fresh Words

Purpose

Students examine and revise word choice in their writing.

Introducing the Activity

Write a short passage on the board that includes some overused, general words, such as:

> Yesterday it rained all day. I played in a baseball game until the eighth inning, and we all got wet. The score was tied, but the game was stopped because it was lightning.

Tell students that writing that consists of common, overused words can appear tired and uninteresting to readers. Ask them to read the passage to themselves, mentally noting at least three verbs or adjectives that might be replaced with stronger, more vibrant word choices.

Using the Graphic Organizer

1. Display a transparency of the graphic organizer on the overhead projector. Then ask students to identify a word from the passage that might be replaced with a stronger word, such as "rained." Write the word on the stem of the first pea pod.

2. Have students brainstorm fresh, lively words that might replace this word (for *rained*, they might suggest *drizzled, poured,* and *sprinkled*). Choose three new words to write on the peas in the pod.

3. Target two more words to use on the other pea pods. Then read the passage aloud. Reread the sentences containing a target word several times, each time replacing that word with a word from the peas. Have students determine if one of the replacement words is more effective than the original word.

4. Rewrite the passage using the more effective words. Then read the passage aloud, inviting students to comment on the difference the new word choices make.

5. Distribute copies of the organizer for students to complete using samples of their own writing. Then have them revise their text using stronger word choices.

Taking It Further

Have students peer-edit a classmate's writing for word choice. When revising, students might use words suggested by their peers to replace ineffective words in their writing.

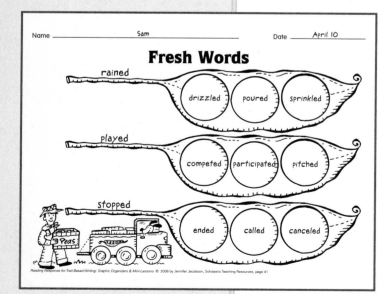

Name _____ Sam _____   Date _____ April 10 _____

Fresh Words

rained — drizzled | poured | sprinkled

played — competed | participated | pitched

stopped — ended | called | canceled

3 Peas

Reading Response for Trait-Based Writing: Graphic Organizers & Mini-Lessons © 2008 by Jennifer Jacobson, Scholastic Teaching Resources, page 41

Fresh Words

Writing Traits

* Ideas
* Voice

Writing Process

* Drafting
* Sharing
* Revising

Literature Link

A Picnic in October by Eve Bunting (Voyager, 2004).

A boy finally understands why his grandmother insists that the family come to Ellis Island each year for the Statue of Liberty's birthday.

Purpose

Students learn the importance of providing quality details in writing.

Introducing the Activity

Explain that authors try to use words that help their audience picture the story as a movie in their minds and feel as if they're actually "in" the movie. Invite students to tell about times they've felt as if they were part of a story they were reading. Ask them to identify ways in which the author brought them into the story.

Using the Graphic Organizer

1. Display the graphic organizer on the overhead projector. Make up a story using 3–4 simple sentences, such as "We went on a picnic. Dad cooked our food. We played. We had lots of fun." Write each sentence on a popcorn bucket.

2. Read the story aloud to students. Ask: *Can you picture the story—what we're eating and playing and why we're having fun? Do you feel like you are there?* Invite students who answer "no" to tell why they don't feel connected to the story. Guide them to understand that the story lacks detail—a critical tool in helping readers visualize events.

3. Work with students to insert details into the story, expanding the existing sentences and adding others to make it more interesting. For instance, you might expand the first sentence to "Yesterday, my family went to the park for a picnic." To "draw" readers into the story, you might add "Runners, dog-walkers, and children stopped to sing songs with us under the shade of a huge oak tree." Write the revised story on the movie screen.

4. Read the revised story aloud. Discuss the differences between the two versions, inviting students to tell why the second version helps readers form a more movie-like picture of the story in their minds.

5. Distribute copies of the organizer for students to use to create their own stories, starting with a few simple sentences on the popcorn buckets.

Taking It Further

When conferencing with students, use the organizer to help them revise their writing to include detail and imagery that appeals to readers.

Name Wendy   Date April 18

You're in the Movie!

Yesterday, my family went to the park for a picnic. Dad grilled hot dogs and hamburgers on our portable grill. Then we tossed a baseball back and forth and had three-legged races. Mom played her guitar when we sat down to rest. Runners, dog-walkers, and children stopped to sing songs with us under the shade of a huge oak tree. We all wanted to come back soon for another wonderful picnic in the park!

Simple Sentence — We went on a picnic.
Simple Sentence — Dad cooked our food.
Simple Sentence — We played.
Simple Sentence — We had lots of fun.

Reading Response for Trait-Based Writing: Graphic Organizers & Mini-Lessons © 2008 by Jennifer Jacobson, Scholastic Teaching Resources, page 43

Name _____

Date _____

You're in the Movie!

Simple Sentence

Simple Sentence

Simple Sentence

Simple Sentence

Writing Traits

❋ Ideas
❋ Organization
❋ Voice
❋ Word Choice
❋ Sentence Fluency
❋ Conventions

Writing Process

❋ Prewriting

Literature Link

Chicken Joy on Redbean Road: A Bayou Country Romp by Jacqueline Briggs Martin (Houghton Mifflin, 2007).

Joe Beebee's music, folks say, will take you up so high, your problems look small enough to stomp on.

Learning From Authors

Purpose

Students examine published works to learn how authors might use specific traits as tools to compose effective stories.

Introducing the Activity

Explain that by examining how authors use the different traits of writing in their craft, students can discover tools that might work for them in their own writing. Then review the six traits of writing with students.

Using the Graphic Organizer

1. Choose a writing trait, such as voice, and a story that clearly demonstrates this trait.

2. Show students the book and explain the reason for your choice. For example, you might say: *I decided to study the use of voice in* Chicken Joy on Redbean Road: A Bayou Country Romp *by Jacqueline Briggs Martin. I noticed that the author used a strong voice in this story and I want to see how she did that.* Write the title and author on the top book on the graphic organizer. Fill in the writing trait on the next book.

3. Read aloud passages that exemplify the writing trait. Then, using the think-aloud method, talk about what you discovered from the text. Say, for example: *Ms. Martin uses repetitive language. She writes, "First I'll gather onions, then the roo." Later she writes, "Onions, potatoes, then the roo." And again, "Onions, potatoes, peppers, then the roo." She makes the story funnier and builds suspense by repeating the same words. I think I could use this tool in my own writing.*

4. On the middle book on the organizer, write page numbers for example text found in the story. Then copy one or more examples on the next book. Write what you learned from the author on the last book.

5. Distribute copies of the organizer. Target a writing trait and provide books that contain clear examples of that trait. Have students choose a book and use what they learn from it to complete the organizer.

Taking It Further

Sort the completed organizers by traits and compile them into a class resource that students can refer to when they need to see concrete and effective examples of the different traits.

Name _____ Kim _____   Date _____ May 23 _____

Learning From Authors

Title: Chicken Joy on Redbean Road: A Bayou Country Romp
Author: Jacqueline Briggs Martin

Writing Trait:
Voice

Page:
10, 14, and 17

Example from book:
"First I'll gather onions, then the roo."
"Onions, potatoes, then the roo."
"Onions, potatoes, peppers, then the roo."

What I learned from the author:
I can repeat language in the text to make my voice stand out.

Trait-Based Writing Graphic Organizers & Mini-Lessons © 2008 by Jennifer Jacobson, Scholastic Teaching Resources, page 45

Name _____   Date _____

Learning From Authors

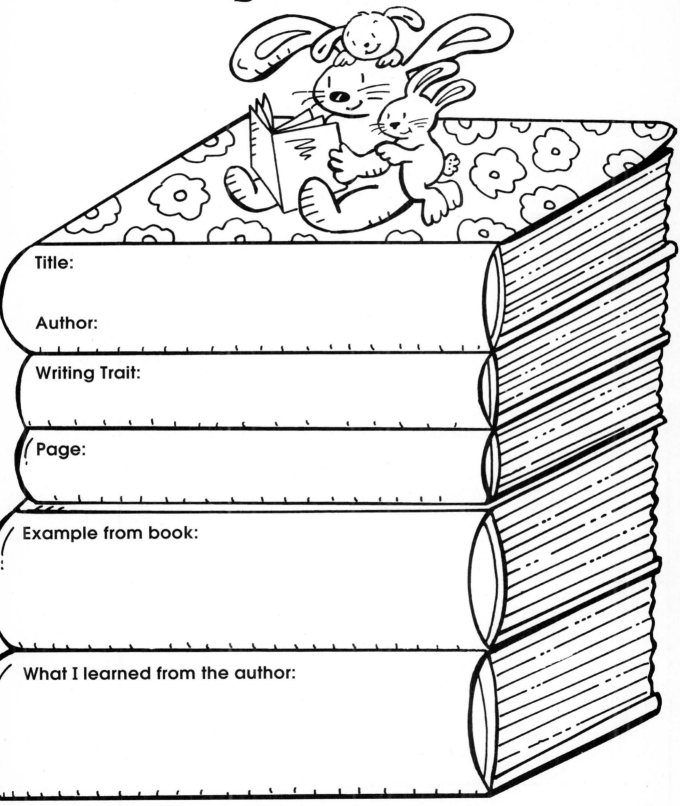

Title:

Author:

Writing Trait:

Page:

Example from book:

What I learned from the author:

Writing Traits

* Ideas
* Organization

Writing Process

* Prewriting
* Drafting
* Revising

Literature Link

Dogs and Cats by Steve Jenkins (Houghton Mifflin, 2007).

This highly engaging flip book examines dogs and cats throughout history, highlighting their physical characteristics, behaviors, and interesting facts.

Leap to New Ideas

Purpose

Students research a topic and organize their information for writing.

Introducing the Activity

To emphasize the importance of using headings to help readers identify the topic of a selection, read aloud several headings found in a children's magazine. Invite students to guess what each article might be about.

Using the Graphic Organizer

1. Display the graphic organizer. Then work with students to brainstorm easy-to-research topics, such as "Dogs," "Weather," and "Airplanes."

2. Select a topic and write it on the first hurdle. Have students brainstorm questions that readers might ask about the topic. Write three questions on the second hurdle.

3. Using the questions as a guide, help students generate possible headings for a paragraph. Write a few headings on the third hurdle.

4. Have students refer to nonfiction books to locate facts about the topic (or you might allow time for them to research other reliable sources, such as the Internet or encyclopedias). Invite them to share their findings and sources. Write five of the facts on a separate sheet of paper, using each one in a complete sentence and citing its source. Then, based on those facts, decide with students if you should use one of the original headings, refine it, or create an entirely new heading to use for your paragraph. Tell them that you'll need a heading that at least three of the facts relate to.

5. After agreeing on a heading, write it and the related facts (in shortened form) on the last hurdle. Explain that you have now narrowed down your topic and gathered and organized information that can be used to write an interesting, concise paragraph.

6. Distribute copies of the organizer for students to use to narrow down a topic and organize information to use in their own writing.

Taking It Further

Have students exchange their paragraphs, fact pages, and organizers with peers. Ask the peers to cross-check each of the sources as they edit the paragraph and provide suggestions for revisions.

Name __Jennifer__   Date __June 3__

Leap to New Ideas

Topics:
Dogs

Questions:
How many dog breeds are there?
Are dogs related to wolves?
How do you take care of a dog?

Heading 1: Dog Breeds
Heading 2: History of Dogs
Heading 3: Caring for a Dog

Finish

Heading: Caring for a Dog

Fact 1:   You should walk your dog every day.

Fact 2:   Your dog needs fresh water and food.

Fact 3:   A dog should be taken to the vet for shots.

Reading Response for Trait-Based Writing: Graphic Organizers & Mini-Lessons © 2008 by Jennifer Jacobson, Scholastic Teaching Resources, page 47

Name _____   Date _____

Leap to New Ideas

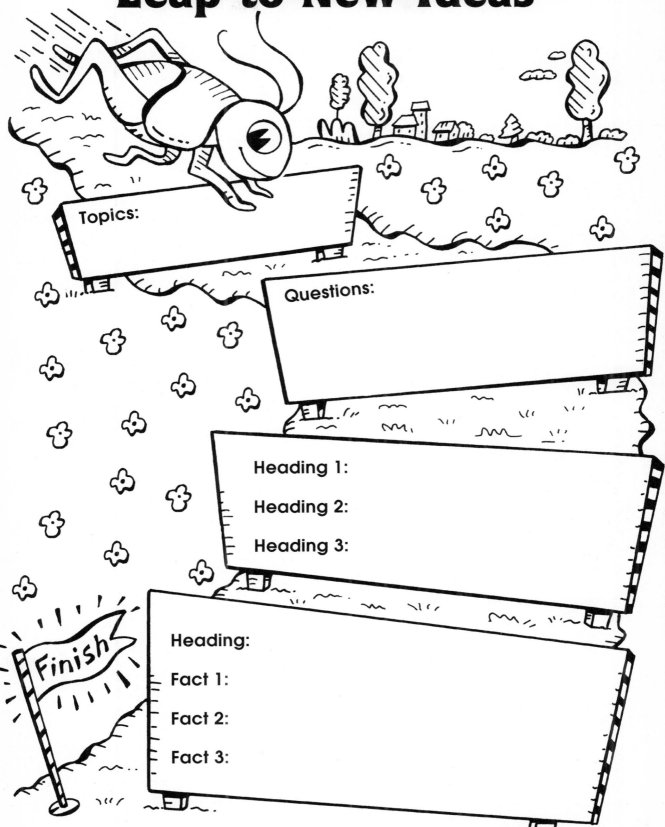

Topics:

Questions:

Heading 1:

Heading 2:

Heading 3:

Finish

Heading:

Fact 1:

Fact 2:

Fact 3:

Notes: